Battle
of the Wolves

Tessy Gold Starry

GOLD STARRY EDITIONS

Print information available on the last page

Rev. date: 10/24/2016

To order additional copies of this book, contact:
Xlibris
0800-056-3182
www.xlibrispublishing.co.uk
Orders@ Xlibrispublishing.co.uk

ADDITIONAL AUTHOR'S NOTES

Battle of the Wolves is a story about childhood and the death of identity and expansiveness of consciousness against the forces of control and manipulation. It deals with an adolescent mind in an adult body changing to adult hood.

The exploration of change is illustrated through a controversial relationship with an older man who acts as a catalyst for the main protagonist to see life in a different way and break away from the forces that have held her back, namely fear and other manipulative devices imposed on her by others.

The story serves as an escape for young children into a fantasy world but also serves as a serious reminder to see things for what they really are and the elements that can hold children, young adults and older adults back in their lives.

It reminds them that even the things we hold most dear can also be extremely destructive. It is a story about the death of innocence and immersion into freedom, physical and psychological freedom but particularly freedom from control, manipulation and fear imposed by others.

It illustrates how children can break negative cycles particularly the cycle of deprivation affecting generation after generation with similar destructive behaviour patterns.

It deals with the battle a young woman endures as she breaks free from familiar bonds holding her back against her will.

Tessy Gold Starry

I want to thank my sisters: Tina McAleer and Mag Casey, Caroline, Mary and Maggie McAleer always with me in spirit and loving me unconditionally, Mary Maghn, Cousin Eileen, Cousin Ann and Debby, Cousin Maureen always with me in spirit , my nieces and nephews: Martina, Shannon, Pearl, Jerry and Willie, Patrick, Theresa and all other Irish family for being a positive support in my life and encouraging me to do what's right for me and for celebrating my art, music, photgraphy and writing.

I would like to thank my Dad, my Mum, my Grandparents in spirit : Harry and Mary Duckworth, Aunt Chris, my brother William and family: Natalie, Rose and Daniel Dixon, dear Margaret Morrissey, dear church friends; Sue and Charles, fellow poet, cook and writer Maria, best and old friends of twenty years: Nick, Ajay, and Henry Fogarty.

Additionally thanks to the clergy and people at Old St Pancras, various groups in Camden: Amy, Claire, Danny, Bryony, Margaret, patient Richard, Joseph Falcone who inspired me to start abstract and surrealist inspired paintings with the acrylic paints I was left by him, Boss VET for rat-cat inspiration, Maurice Dominic Mary Walsh for his great insight into life, Sergio Bezzanti and his awesome creativeness, contribution, enthusiasm and support with some of the graphics in this novel, Liz head teacher of Guardian Angels Primary School, fellow writers: Chris Bird, Ruth, Ricky, Conrad, Jim Morrison, Boss Bishop Poet, Romina, David Olsen a wonderfully inspiring poet and good friend, Morag Styles, (my tutor at Cambridge University during my MPHIL: Critical Approaches to Children's Literature) Gold Dust Writers mentor Sally Cline and to everyone that has supported me in my writing, art, music, photography or offered me inspiration over the years.

Additionally, those few people that have offered me unconditional love in my life including my two cats Georgie 0' Miley and Sangiovese Apricot without which I wouldn't have been able to have the confidence to progress, flourish and grow.

I also want to acknowledge some of my favourite authors, the Abstract Expressionism movement in New York , inspiration taken from The Abstract and Surrealist Artists,

Postmodern contemporary picture book authors, African freedom fighters and musicians.

These have all been great sources of inspiration for me but in particularly:A.A Milne, George Orwell, C.S Lewis, Lewis Carroll, Keats, Charles Dickens, Michael Rosen, Michael Morpurgo, Shakespeare, Nelson Mandala, Charlie Pride, Dolly Parton, Emily Gravitz, Van Morrison, Sir Paul McCartney and John Lennon for encouraging love, peace and liberation world values, that resonate with me.

nce upon a time

there was a beautiful princess and an old, clever king.

They both lived in separate, beautiful and powerful kingdoms where emeralds and rubies were a plenty and beautiful food grew from the silvery, birch trees and the great oak trees.

The oak trees their leaves whispered and their gnarled endless roots bore deep, rich secrets wise and grandeur standing witness to the lives of the beautiful princess and the clever, old King.

They lived in the age of fairy tales so anything was possible and dragon wars often tried to rule and conquer both of their kingdoms. But they had something else in common.

Both the old King and the Princess had witnessed cruel and difficult times in their childhood. They had tyrannical fathers. The old King as a  young boy had struggled with his father who would drink many an ale and beat his mother. The rest of the time he was spoiled so ended up very confused with these two extremes. One thunderous day his father tried to stab him and his mother so the Old King had grown fierce and ruthless as he defended his mother like a wolf defends his wolf pups.

The young princess' father had been robbed of something very precious when he was young and had grown over protective exerting control through fear manipulation, guilt and creating dependencies. He also was successful and used strategy, talent and charm to climb up the tallest glimmering castles, palaces and mansions. As the years went by his cruelty grew as he forgot his humble roots and sense of humility.

As the days, weeks and years passed both the King and Princess grew fierce and their soft hearts broke time and time again. They both had a burning energy of fire within them, that if ignited, could produce the largest flames even the most dangerous, volatile dragon could not match.

However, the old king had also become very clever over the passage of time and had learnt how to capture every part of the world through strategy and charm. The princess had learnt how to cope through turning to artistic talents and her physical appearance - all of which were colourful and striking to the world.

So it was the princess succeeded and advanced in her kingdom - but not entirely. She didn't know how to strategize or plan for different situations particular situations with ferocious or deceitful dragons or witches in disguise.

She also didn't understand herself fully as if a part of her emotions had dried up in childhood, like a baby's tears ebbing away through the cold, lost night.

The princess was unhappy and lonely. She was so used to fighting dragons and her tyrannical father that any marriage suitors presented to her seemed boring and as the weeks passed by an oppressive, inane mist started gathering at her palace window.

One day, the clever, old king and the beautiful princess met by chance, in a dark, tangly forest where the tree roots curled and hissed while the tree trunks stood majestic, their elegant silvery branches stretching up to the heavens.

The fight in both the old King and the beautiful Princess fought hard and strong - physically, intellectually, psychologically and emotionally. They battled. They debated. They embraced. They devoured. Like the battle of two wolves each strong with its own energy and force.

The Princess in her youth and innocence didn't understand why this was happening but she was really drawn to the clever, old King despite the age gap and different kingdoms in which they lived.

One day, the clever, old, King was sorting through his things and his magic tools. The princess noticed he had some extremely glittery magic tools, some of which he wouldn't let her see or touch. But even the smallest of these magic tools she was drawn to and she didn't know why.

She felt like she could see the world differently in ways that she hasn't seen before... Very slowly it felt like this magic was making her see everything more clearly including problems with her father.

One night the princess crept out of the bed in which they both lay quietly so the old king didn't hear her and stumbled upon a box.

In the gold box lay a bright, silver, pearly pair of sparkling glasses and next to it was a lace pure, white handkerchief. What on earth would she do with these she thought?

Another night she crept downstairs when the King was sound asleep and put on the glasses and pushed the silken handkerchief to her soft nose. It smelt of roses and sweet pollen but in the next sniff it smelt of decay and dust. The princess sneezed. What on earth was going on? And what were these for?

Silently she crept up to the window and gazed outside. Suddenly a star fell from the sky and told her that she could still fight but in ways that were more subtle she had never seen before, let alone had to use.

She thanked the star gratefully and helped him back into the soft, glittering sky. The moon sky and clouds all assisted one beautiful evening. The star was so grateful that in return he told all his friends and the night sky glittered and shone so bright the princess cried out with pure delight and happiness.

The world though brighter and gleaming through the glasses seemed easier to tackle.

The Princess could see the dark wolves on the horizon and the evil dragons hiding under their cloaks that she never saw before.

Wolf picture charcoal with orange eyes inserted here to create dramatic impact

Even the most friendliest of dragons that she had previously trusted looked different when she wore the glasses. She now saw the horrid glint in their charm and deception that she could not see before.

She had trusted these dragons and dined with them confessing her deepest secrets. Terrified, anxiety crept and raced through her.

But what was the purpose of the handkerchief you ask? The lace handkerchief helped to warn the princess about situations to come. When people could be trusted it smelt of rose and when there was doubt or danger the smell changed to decay waste and the smell of blood.

The princess, her senses sharpened with the magic that left an invisible rainbow powder behind her grew steadily more empowered.

She was also very frightened with her new found knowledge and wisdom and played her harp deep in her palace walls and read and wrote poetry to escape from her new found discoveries. A smoke bear once appeared in her palace. She wasn't sure what to do with it but thanked it for appearing incase she needed a cuddle. It looked like a teddy she once had called," Big Ted."

Deep down she felt foolish for not knowing for so many dark and long years. A piece of her innocence and childhood disappeared one night in a sad lilac mist circling swiftly away from her as quick as a lost memory then shattering through the waves of time.

However - just as fast as the princess learnt about herself she learnt about her glittering world and people around her.

She had a soft loving side that made all her male squires fall in love with her. She had not realised this however but still longed for a genuine meeting of: minds, experience, love and care with a hint of darkness. A fiery soul mate. Some of her squires were so sweet and kind to her but something was missing...

For the first time in a long time the clever old King was in a situation that he hasn't encountered either.

For decades he strategised his way out of situations and made even the fieriest of evil dragons cackle with laugher whilst stealing their treasure. He had stolen the beautiful mistresses' hearts with promises of riches which of course, he had no intention of sharing.

The King had given no value to people's time yet fought to keep his own time and punished cruelly for any rejections with ferocious, tormenting, anger that made the whole kingdom dark and without light or heat for a year. Even some of the stars fell out of the sky with fear and deepest sorrow during this turbulent melancholy. But every time the king rejected someone a part of himself fell away and perished.

However - as the days passed the a bubbling energy between both the Princess and the old King grew to the strongest bond ever and had electric, heavenly and death like qualities.

The old King screamed and yelled hurtling his tools round the castle garden, carving axes and sharpening the blades on his shed doors trying to hide in his wood work making new wooden doors to barricade out his thoughts.

Any unfortunate goblins that happened to be lurking in the castle bushes were thrown with all his strength into the nearby futile forests. They would never be seen again. People could hear their cries as savaged thieves would spring on their bruised, defenceless bodies.

The King wasn't used to these strong feelings and sought ways to dominate and control the Princess like past princesses, mistresses and scarlet, fire breathing dragons.

The King's largest desire and need was as vast as his biggest fear. He hid it away in a tiny corner of his mind and refused to give it time and attention. He longed for similar things deep down: a sacred meeting of minds, psychologically emotionally and intellectually but knew that dominating someone was easier for him. He also enjoyed domination. He was a tyrant.

Every week, the beautiful princess wrote the old King letters and found poems from deep in her heart because she longed to connect with him. But he hid away from her love, frightened after the sad, tragic years of his life and tried to create difficult situations.

He refused to read her letters or drink any wine, fearful his heart strings would stir and awaken. He was scared of his heart. It might prevent him from galloping away on his horse and never coming back.

In actual fact the King was being drawn back to the beautiful princess each time, frustrated and annoyed, throwing his rusty tools down on the ground in a weary heap like an old stick ready to break.

Her youthful spirit and energy was vibrant but he was tired and needed rest within his castle. The creases on his face started to unfold and deepen into deep crevasses. He couldn't keep up and longed to sleep but her magic was unrelenting. Exhausting. Addictive.

The days, weeks and months of his life gone by hidden in these folds were growing steadily wearier.

Time ticked turbulently in both their kingdoms but as each took small steps to move away their hearts were full of longing and their minds full of desire. A desire so strong it could overwhelm and delight to the highest level whilst also seeking to dominate and blind all with a single blink.

The clever, old King feared emotional intimacy because with it, came vulnerability and he desperately wanted to conquer the princess. He was furious and threw himself into his work. In one day he had carved the wood for doors of twenty four palaces working day and night until he crumpled, a heap on his bed. He had no need of pillows just a bare, lonely place on which to lay his tiresome bones. His bones were ready to crack. With his soul.

The old kings desire to see the princess was not just hungry but were ravenous starving wolves aching, the Battle of two wolves trying to draw close but scared of what might happen. The clever old King tried strategies that he had used before with previous princesses and innocent maidens but they didn't work.

He looked at his old dusty maps for routes through the vibrant kingdom that would surprise her but her warmth seem to melt his inner bitterness. It melted his need to control and in its place came a guilty feeling. A sadness and a desire to do good.

Despite the King battling with his feelings he continued to lay traps for the princess every day and refused to give her answers. He tried to win her over with tantalising, tempting, twinkles and sparks that resided in his eyes. The girl resisted these as she could smell his cruelty. It was dark like death and blood. She also didn't understand why she resisted and fought him so hard.

She darted aside, resisted, tumbled over, got up, righted herself - yet every step more clear, more powerful, more insightful.

In a moment of angry passion she yelled at the old king, the words tumbling and rushing,"You can run from me old man for one week, three weeks or five. But I will always be haunting you in your heart and head." She leapt about the furniture in her palace with a youthful energy and spontaneity that deeply unsettled the old king.

The old King knew his tricks were running out and every time he uttered something he gave a part of himself away, unknowingly.

He searched and searched. I need to find a way to run away from this beautiful princess he thought. She is turning my life upside down and her energy will dig my grave. I know he dug deep into his thoughts I will lull her into a false sense of security and then depart for ever in pursuit of an easier life! He plotted. He schemed. He pondered. He stalked the shadows in his castle pouncing on the smallest of cracks.

Meanwhile back in the princesses kingdom one beautiful, magnetic, starry night the princess had a dream. The old King had told her everything started in dreams. It was of a vision of the two of them living in his grand sparkling, golden castle.

In her dream she remembered that the his castle was large and once upon an Autumnal season, the two had shared hot tasty meals there washed down with ice cold water retiring in front of the cosy fire, the flakes hissing and spitting yet laughing and dancing in the background.

Outside of the castle walls had been a relaxing, blissful green where they had found quiet spaces to chat and hide under the trees sipping and laughing away time in the warmest sun rays.

Drinking wine from large goblets in the local village inns haunted her fondest memories and then sleeping soundly like a baby the purest form of bliss.

It was a wonderful escape from the worlds' perils: forbidding dragons and ghostly figures who sometimes used to stand watching her wistfully at her window in the dead of night. Like a soul suddenly taken and not laid to rest.

In the past the princess used to leave candles burning throughout the night and called on the stars for their warmth and light protection and company. Protection from wistful but gentle spirits who longed to engage with her who missed and loved her. However this sweet bliss commanded the lights off and bright harmony filled the air.

How safe she felt here in her dream so the very next day after waking she swiftly rode her black horse to the Kings Kingdom and whispered to the old King, " If I give you enough love and kindness from my heart will you feel safe enough to let me into your heart and life?"

"Never!" roared the King.

He had become so used to domination and control. "If you reject me, ten times will I blight you," the words running in terror from his mouth with a flash of thunder and a crash of lightening the whole path shook and lit up the gates of hell.

The Princess knew he would do this and could be thrown to the other side of the kingdom with no mercy, half dead, black and blue, beyond ruin.

She uttered from her heart pure, earnestly, cautiously and with courage,

"Can we find a way to make this work, to bring each other happiness? If we part and don't pursue this there will always be an ache. I accept you - will you give me your heart? "

The old kings heart was ancient and dusty like him and he had forgotten what it was like to love and be loved and enjoyed being safely locked away in his grand castle away from hurt and pain. He had got used to his freedom and liked to ride out into the night returning at dawn. The shy moon and stars bearing witness to his where-bouts.

Legend had it that when the old, clever king finally did return home to sleep of a night in his dark castle, his snores were one of a wolf and his breath snarled around his teeth like a raging, injured animal lying in wait. What for, you ask?

I'm not sure the old king always knew but he always found something to hunt meanwhile on a dusty shelf his heart once fresh, withered away out of reach.

Some days he longed for his heart back staring with piercing, blue eyes and a mop of glorious, silvery hair.

The old King did not give the princess his heart. He could not reach it. He would not reach it. It was locked away in a dark box.

Every day and night he cried inside. He clutched at his pain, like the holes in his heart. The holes in the castle tapestries hung round his castle each stitch falling like a lost year yearning for happiness.

But one fine, bright day the old King looked out of his castle, his blue eyes searching, questioning, gazing, wondering the green parks in front of him . He knew time was running out. He had to see the beautiful princess!

Quick as a flash he blundered and bounded out of the rusty, neglected castle walls where many a rusty tool was strewn - the horses hooves pounding and shaking the ground and breaking earth beneath him so fast he nearly collided with a witch from the village.

"Where are you going in such a hurry?" she enquired with curiosity and a sneer."To see the Princess I missed so much," said the old king, "desperate to get on his way and past this interfering, old hag. But she is married," replied the witch, with a smile on her face. The witch loved to see pain. Destruction was her middle name.

The old king jumped off his horse in a flash and knocked the witch to the ground in one swoop of his fist. That will teach you to laugh at me he bellowed with a fast, furious and fuming brow. The witch disappeared into a puff of green smoke and he was left. Alone.

And then a very strange thing happened-just as the old King recovered his fist a sparrow whispered in the old kings ear and then hastily took his leave.

The king stumbled back against the wall surprised at what the sparrow had told him.

After a few minutes the King composed himself and repeated the sparrows words out loud, "Go and find the Princess you desire. Her husband is now dead and you can claim her for your own."

Suddenly, it is my chance the thoughts raced and shoved and without further hesitation the clever old king leapt on his horse galloping across the forbidden, rustling marshes.

He rode like never before, the wind crashing and lashing through his hair a fiery God like energy pushing him through dark mountain and vale. Galloping back the years of his life. Clawing back the dreams that were wildly thrashing in front of him, just out of reach...

The old King arrived at the princess's glittering, cosy palace and peered inside. He had bought a solid, gold ring to bind the love between them so it never went astray again.

But on the floor, her dark hair curled around her, ivory shining skin, the princess lay. The cold stone floor her lips red and ripe yet fading. Dead.

However, in the princesses place stood a fair maiden, identical but with fair hair and a wise look in her eyes. The fair version of the princess stood gazing down at the body. "That part of me is gone," she uttered.

"But how can there be two of you?" demanded the King. "I'm not sure," she answered," but a part of me has died for ever."

No sooner had the King looked, the fair maiden jumped on a silver horse and rode away into the forest. Gone and far from the King's reach and all others like him with a fresh energy free to pursue all the delights of the world and utilize all her brilliant talents in the best possible way.

Her crown shone with merriment, each jewel representative of a different quality of her. Red for passion, silver for masculinity, purple for wisdom, pink for femininity and empowerment of women and blue for talent.

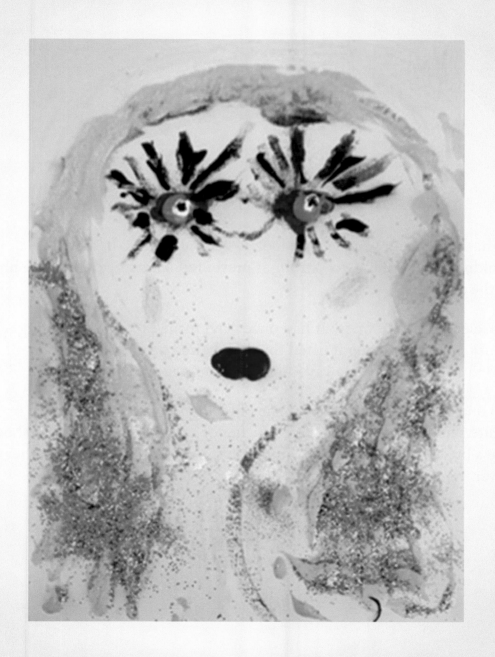

Aghast. The King stopped. He looked back at his life. In a flash. He couldn't cry. A feeling, too strong it prevented tears forcefully froze him to the spot.

The electricity and fire that had once been turned to tears, a wailing frantic ocean so strong it lifted the dark haired princesses body up off the floor and down stream away into a dark but peaceful oblivion.

No one ever heard from or saw the old King again. Many a knight or squire said they sometimes saw a flicker of a candle of light in his abode like a breath here then gone. Similar to the princess and the love they never managed to share.

Now their best secrets lie with God in heavenly bliss. A bright sweet ray of their love shining from the darkest and lightest parts of the sky. A dream away, as everything starts in your dreams.

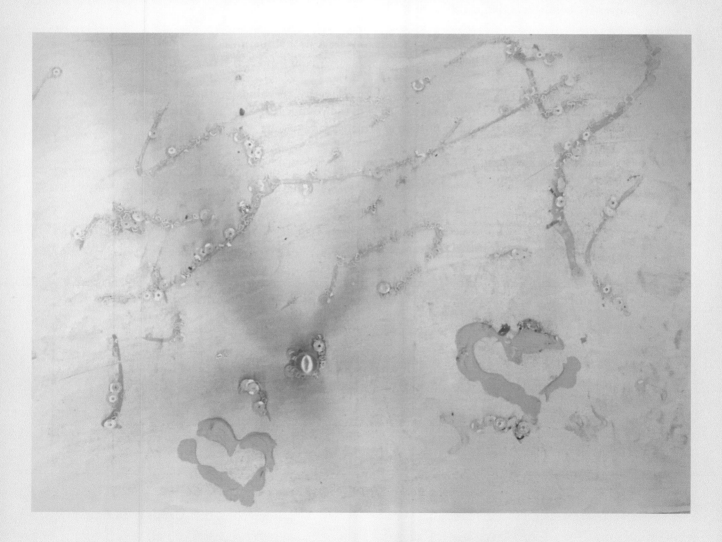

ADDITIONAL AUTHOR'S NOTES:

As a child I always believed in happy endings and the power of positivity and love and strength in life and death (as emotions are timeless) but especially in the face of evil, adversity, coldness and injustice.

I hope my books inspire children and adults to believe in their happy endings; free from anything that holds them back.

This positive spirit lives on in me today in spirit, narrative, teaching and the special friendships and life that I'm blessed to have. I'm the youngest of fifteen and I'm very happy to say we are all alive today even if there is a thirty year age gap.

We never know how long we have but to attempt to follow our dreams in the time we are blessed to have is important for every one.

Many people don't even try to follow their dreams because they are victims of mind control created through subtle forms of manipulation, creation of dependencies and other strategies some people choose to use in a negative way for their own gain and insecurities.

I believe all of this stands in the way of an individual realizing their potential just as much as financial, educational disadvantages and prejudice. Some times people are not even aware of the opportunities that passed them by and are blind blocked or resistance to the deliberate deceptions.

I encourage everyone to pursue their dreams and see the people holding them back. I believe we need to be brave enough to see things for what they are, not what we want them to be however hard.

I believe this means attempting to step out of our circumstances and limitations: financial, psychological, emotional, social- economic, educational, physical and the fears, control systems and ideologies imposed on us ideally taking the best bits of everything and removing the rest.

My books portray dark challenging themes with predators which are deliberately confronting to remind children of all the dangers particularly the ones close to them that they might be blind to. I'm hoping to provoke children and adults into questioning the world around them in order to make healthier choices for them as individuals and provide a stimulating but " safe" experience for children to experience fear through fictional escapism.

I believe childhood and life is an extremely special. Children and adults should be able to feel free and live without psychological fears and threat. Insecurities can become normalized within destructive relationships and I challenge people to wake up to these undermining behaviors. This is made easier with forms of unconditional love, healing and full acceptance in childhood or late adulthood.

In making positive changes I believe we can allow others to make other changes as I believe we all connected. I hope my books open children to the fears that hold them back, so they become healthy liberated adults who can be happy and encouraging of others with mindful awareness, generous communications free of envy; competition and compromising hurtful behaviors that can be harmful to others.

Admittedly these are some what idyllic ideas but if enough people believed in them they would probably manifest more fully in society, which would benefit everyone.

I hope my books and art encourage fresh independent thinking with their different perspectives and interpretations that challenge stereo types ultimately creating degrees of liberation and happiness in children and adults who are open to the concepts in the book, even if it challenges their current perceptions.

Printed in the United States
By Bookmasters